Bigger Than Me

Monyetta Shaw

Library of Congress Cataloging-in-Publication Data
Monyetta Shaw
Bigger Than Me
Edited by: Driadonna Roland
Photography by: DeWayne Rogers
Cover Design by: NickRichGFX, LLC
Published by: Evan Grace Publishing, LLC: Atlanta, GA

ISBN: 978-0692667262
10 9 8 7 6 5 4 3 2 1
Printed in the United States of America

Note: This book is intended only as a real life testimony of the life and times of Monyetta Shaw. Readers are advised to consult a professional before making any changes in their life. The reader assumes all responsibility for the consequences of any actions taken based on the information presented in this book. The information in this book is based on the author's research and experience. Every attempt has been made to ensure that the information is accurate; however, the author cannot accept liability for any errors that may exist. The facts and theories about life are subject to interpretation, and the conclusions and recommendations presented here may not agree with other interpretations.

Table of Contents

Introduction

In life we go through some things that can make us or break us. We have a choice about how we will handle every situation. We can fold or we can stand strong and keep going. I made a decision to keep going. Most little girls had visions of their wedding day, their first home, their kids, and their life goals. I was one of those little girls. Then I became one of those women who get so close and then lose it. I have my beautiful kids, my health and strength. Some could say that's all that matters. Truthfully, I agree with that but the things I lost also hurt really bad.

I'm writing this book with the hopes that my story, my struggles, and my strength will help you find your strength. My hope is that you will turn your pain into purpose as well. It's easiest to throw in the towel and quit, but there is something divine about pressing forward despite all that has happened to you. I hope you can see my heart in this book. I'm not perfect, nor do I pretend to be. I'm human and I make mistakes, but I own up to my mistakes. At the same time, I'm also human enough to fall for lies, games, and deceit. I have to own up to that as well.

I hope you can gain some valuable lessons from my story. Please don't judge me because I've done enough of that myself. If anything, pray for me. I hope we all find peace and fully heal from the pain of our past. I know it won't be easy but I know it's possible. Take your time reading this book and make sure you let every lesson soak in. If you're open to growing with me then I'm positive this book will help you accomplish that goal. I don't know what's possible but it's my hope that we can move past the rain and find the gold at the end of the rainbow.

Let's grow together. There is no need to wait any longer. There is no need to hurt and suffer any longer. Happiness is a choice and it's your right to make that choice. Choose happiness today.

CHAPTER I

Save Some of You for You

I gave it all up. I did the most. I did more than the average woman would do for love. I left it all there. I'm fighting right now for my sanity. Writing this book is therapy. Just when you think you're fine, you're hit with another blow. This book was going in a totally different direction, and in the midst of writing it I was hit by blow after blow. I will not discuss all of the blows but just enough so that you will get the point. The blows knocked me down and I'm getting back up right now. I'm standing, barely standing. I'm hurting. I'm angry. But I'm not going to let either of those emotions control me. I have to find a way to heal, to learn, and to grow.

I met my ex at a time in my life when I thought I knew myself. I was smart, classy, funny, and outgoing. I was on my way to doing big things in my life. Then I fell in love. I fell in love before I knew what real love felt like, looked like, or anything else. I was blindsided by love. I can't say I didn't want it. I can't say I didn't enjoy the good times and gain strength in the bad times. I loved it and I wouldn't change it because from it came my two biggest joys in life, my children. I just didn't know what I was doing.

I had no reason to doubt a man. I had no reason to be bitter, spiteful, or have my guards up too high. I was hoping that I would get out of life what I put in. I was hoping that I would attract someone who had my same heart and morals. I attracted his potential, but I couldn't bring it out. I couldn't force him to grow up. I couldn't force him to be faithful. I couldn't force him to change. The lifestyle of the rich and famous had more power than I did. The lure of the thirst traps was stronger than me. I did everything I could do to keep my man and I still lost.

I learned a valuable lesson through it all and that's why I'm starting the book off with this chapter because right now it's echoing louder than anything else in my mind. You have to know who you are and you have to save some of you for you. You can't give all of you to someone who hasn't given all of themselves to you. You can't sacrifice everything you are and put all your dreams on hold if they aren't 100% committed to you and the family you're trying to build. You can't hold onto their lies and sweet nothings whispered during pillow talk. You have to be careful. I'm not saying to be bitter, judgmental, or to sabotage a relationship. I'm saying take your time and make sure the person you're dealing with is the real deal and not just a decoy.

I put everything out there. I changed who I was as a person. I lost myself. I lost my self-esteem. I lost my self-worth. I lost my self-respect. I started grappling for anything I could do to keep the life that we'd built. I was making plans with a hope strategy. I didn't have any wedding vows. I had a ring but I didn't have a real commitment. I was beginning to think that this wouldn't last forever after all. I just kept telling myself it would just so I could stay focused and keep working toward it.

As women we come in with all these high hopes. We believe that we can change a man. We believe we can be the one who turns his life around. We can, but not every man, and not just any man. We can only do that for a man who is willing to meet us halfway. A man has to know who he wants to be as a father and a husband, not just as a businessman. If he doesn't buy into true growth, it won't work. You'll be wasting your time and losing your mind along the way. I had to learn the hard way. I believed every word and I held onto it. I was gullible and naïve, but I didn't know that going into the relationship. I found out along the way like many women do. I got to a point of no return. Once I had my first child, I didn't want to turn back. I've always dreamed of being married with kids. I didn't want to be a single mom. I grew up in a loving two-parent home where I saw great examples growing up. I wanted to be that great example. There was something in me that made me want to make it work no matter what.

I subconsciously started turning a blind eye to the lies and infidelity. It hurt me but I was masking the pain. I wore a smile even when underneath I was in tears. I pretended that everything was OK, but really I was hurting on the inside. I tried to befriend my nice purses, shoes, and cars, but I realized that none of those things loved me back or kept me warm at night. I did everything I could do to keep myself in shape and pretty. I worked out, ate right, and took care of myself. I wanted to be perfect but I kept falling short. I started to compare myself to the other girls who would get all of his attention. I was losing it.

What could I do? What type of sacrifices could I make to please my man? I was searching. I was desperate. I began condoning the cheating basically. I started telling myself that all men cheat and that it's just the way of the world. There are so many other women being cheated on, I said. No man is completely faithful for life, I said. I was telling myself whatever I had to just to get by each day.

So one day I begged him to be honest. I told him that I never wanted any girl, any thot, or any jumpoff to ever have one up on me — for her to be able to walk into a room, laugh, and say that she has my man. That was a huge problem. I was forced to compare myself to these girls. No woman should ever have to do that! But now because his actions awakened my insecurities, there I was desperately trying to hold on to my man by any means necessary, so I thought. And what I am about to reveal next is the lowest of the low. I basically told him that if he was going to cheat he should tell me first and please use protection. Why would I ever say that? I was dying inside. I just knew that this was a phase and he would soon grow out of it or realize just how wrong it is and want to stop.

Sounds crazy right? But maybe not too crazy once you keep reading. I basically lost my everlasting mind! I cried and talked until I was blue in the face, but nothing worked, not even my drastic measures. Nothing stopped the games and the lies. The crazy thing about it is that I never thought about retaliating. I wasn't raised to degrade myself in any way. If I would have tipped out to sleep with another man that would have hurt me just as bad as it would have hurt him. I couldn't hurt myself by trying to hurt him. It wasn't worth it. I know two wrongs don't make a right, so I was just looking for something right that would make it right.

I was already defiling the bedroom by not being married, but now I was willing to take another step: a threesome. I wasn't a prude when it came to the man I loved, but thinking back I must say that I am not proud of this part of my truth. I wanted to prove that I was just as sexy and willing as the other women. I told myself that if I weren't in it then another woman would be taking my place. I wanted to show him that I was a rider, his other gun, the Bonnie to his Clyde. I'd always dreamed of being a wife but here I found myself being treated almost like a glorified jumpoff. Never did I think that I wasn't enough for a man.

I've since learned that some men are willing to give away years of their life to a woman just to pass time. Some men use women for their ego, image, or brand, but never have any intentions to be real with that woman. I thought what I had was real. I'm finding out by the day just how fake it was. The only things real are the two lives brought into the world. It hurts me to think that my actions as their mother could one day hurt them in a way that I can't repair. That's what I think hurts most mothers in my shoes. We give so much for love and we sacrifice everything and end up lonely and lost. I don't have a choice but to be strong. I have to get back up and stay up. I have to fight for my kids' well-being. I have to be the mother they need.

CHAPTER 2

Healing From the Pain

What is pain? We don't really understand it, but yet we feel it. It can break us down, but can it build us up? We go through life getting hurt over and over again and we always find ourselves getting back up, dusting off, and looking for the strength to carry on. Life can be so hard at times. Sometimes it's hard to believe that healing is even possible. We hide the pain oh so well. We put on a smile even when we're crying inside. We walk around with our heads held high but really we don't feel like getting out of bed. I know that pain. I live with that pain.

It's not easy and I'm not sure it ever will be, but I keep going. It's bigger than me.

I want you to think about the pain that you'd feel if you put all of your hopes and dreams into a person and then one day they decide they're going to move on without you. I didn't see it coming. I sacrificed my life, my dreams, my mind, my body, my spirit, and everything else I could give. I was thinking "we" while he was thinking "me." Just like any little girl I remember dreaming of one day being a wife. I could see my dress as I was walking down the aisle. I could see the smile on my parents' faces. I knew that it would be beautiful. I saw the traditional life my parents had and I knew in my heart that I would have that life too. I was sadly mistaken. I was taken for granted. I was left hanging. I tell myself all the time that I know I wasn't perfect, but I know I didn't deserve this. If I'd cheated on him I could understand this being the consequences. If I'd talked down to him and wished bad upon him, I could understand this being the consequences. Instead I was going along trying to find a way to make him happy. I was trying to find a way to please him so that we could spend the rest of our lives together. I have two kids from a relationship that I hoped would last forever.

What did I do wrong? Maybe it's my fault for having sex before marriage. Maybe it's my fault for trusting in man instead of God. Maybe it's my fault for giving too much of myself too soon. Maybe it's my fault for being down for whatever and not maintaining my self-respect and dignity in the relationship. Maybe it's my fault. I'm not sure if you've ever blamed yourself but I do believe it's only human to ask those questions. I believe that it's good to ask those questions so that you can accept responsibility for the role you may have played in the situation, but it's not right to blame yourself. I can't blame myself for his shortcomings. I can't blame myself for being lied to and misled. I can't blame myself. I can only be accountable for my actions. I have to pick up and keep moving. I have to know that it was beyond myself and I just wasn't what he wanted at the end of the day. I don't know who or what got into his head and why it turned out the way it did, but it did.

Then to add insult to injury, I had to watch the man I wanted to marry run off and get married to someone else. Imagine that. Imagine giving your everything to a man and having not just one, but two of his kids, then being left out of the blue and having to watch him ride off into the sunset with another woman. Imagine having to read about their wedding online and see pictures of them together. It burns. It stings. It hurts. That is the type of pain I'm talking about.

This pain runs deep because this isn't a normal relationship. I will have to read about my ex in magazines. I will have to watch him on TV. I will have to listen to him on the radio. I get tagged in their pictures on social media every day. Even when I'm not listening to him, I'm listening to his work. I also have to see her; a woman who I can't hate, a woman who I don't really know, a woman who I can't blame. I would be her too; any woman would. We all want love and if a man is going to give it to us, we're going to take it no matter the cost. She will have everything that I ever wanted with the same man that I wanted it with. Imagine being subbed out of your life and having to watch another woman live your dreams. Those are the thoughts I have to fight on a daily basis. She will be the stepmother. Her heart won't have to be fully invested in them like mine is but yet her opinion of them will hold weight. Her influence in his life will influence my kids' lives whether I like it or not. So often this is how it goes, and this is something that I have to heal from. This is where the pain runs deep.

I can't carry this pain. I can't let this pain weigh me down and keep me down. I have no other choice but to heal because again, this is bigger than me. I was feeling OK and I was making my way, then one thing after another starts to happen and you wonder if you can heal and keep going. You wonder, what's next? First it's the breakup. Then he wants to be monogamous now but with someone he just met. Then they are engaged, then pregnant after we both promised to get procedures done because we already had our boy and our girl and we didn't want anymore. Then it's watching them get married and start this new life. I was pulling my hair asking God, *Why me?*

Maybe you can heal in private but I have to heal publicly. I have to wear my strength where everyone can see it. I can be going to the grocery store and people are looking to see if I'm broken. I have to straighten my back and lift my head. I have to stand strong and keep going. Pain has a funny way of making us stronger. Pain is a healing agent, it's been said. You have to admit to the pain to heal it. If you pretend that nothing bothers you and you run from the feelings then you never process them and get ahold of them. I could tell you that nothing bothers me and that seeing them ride off into the sunset doesn't bother me but who would I be fooling? We know pain when we see it. You're a human just like I am and you know that what I'm going through has to hurt. So what would it benefit me to lie about my pain? I have to admit to it. I have to confront the pain. I have to feel it so I can heal it. Our minds will naturally kick in and bring healing if we confront our issues head on. I know I'll be OK. Every day is better than the last by the grace of God. I know I'll meet the man for me and I'll know better next time. That's why I'm so cautious as I start to date. I'll see the red flags and I won't ignore them.

I was just at a seminar and the speaker was talking about healing before dealing. He was talking about how we have to get to the point where we can love like we've never been hurt before. We have to be 100% happy being single before we are ready to be in a relationship. I don't think he meant literally 100% happy but he meant content and OK with it enough to not be desperate for love. I know I need that day to come. I know it will come and I'll have to keep moving toward it. I realize that it won't be easy. I'll have setbacks. I pray he never tries to come back. I don't know what I'd do. I hear about that often when a man moves on and is with his new woman but still trying to tiptoe back into his ex's life. I pray that's never me. I know I'll meet some lames while trying to heal, but my real hope is that I don't push away a good guy because of the pain that bums caused.

I'm wondering what would it take to fully heal. I know they say that time heals all things but I also believe we have to do some work during that time. I'll touch on that later in the book to share what I'm doing while I'm healing.

I want you to think about your pain. What is holding you down? What is holding you back? Will you continue to let it hurt you? Will you continue to wallow in that situation? That's what we have to ask ourselves. We deserve to love and be loved. We deserve peace and happiness. But we have to love ourselves enough to know that. Then we have to get up and do something about it. It's not enough to just say it. We have to do something.

I'm not sure how long the pain will linger. I'm not sure what things will trigger my pain to flare back up. I know it'll be a battle, but I'm ready to fight for my peace of mind. I'm already at a point where I don't cry at night. I can get up and get out and function. I'm going out with my friends. I go to seminars. I spend a lot of fun time with my kids. I'm starting to date a bit. I'm not dead in the water. I'm not in bed all day moping. So I realize that my resilience has already kicked it. You have to kick it in so you don't lose your mind. It's all about what you tell yourself. In order for me to heal I have to realize that I didn't lose the man of my dreams. I lost a headache. I learned a lesson. This lesson will make me bigger, better, and stronger. That's what I have to constantly remind myself of.

I notice a lot of people make the mistake of feeling like what they lost is what they need. But if you lost it, then it wasn't meant to be yours. What's for you is for you and nothing or no one can stop that. I didn't lose mine. Instead, she gained hers. Well Lord knows I thought it was mine too until life happened. But a part of healing is moving forward and not wishing bad on anyone. You have to be focused on yourself and your life. You have to move forward for you and you can't worry about someone else's karma or even about them at all. Get up and get out and go get your dreams.

My focus now is to not let my pain affect anything else in my life. So I don't want my pain to cause me to neglect my kids. That is never an option. I don't want my pain to cause me to forsake my dreams. I want to take this thing in stride and build on it. I want to gain wisdom from this experience. I want the pain to make me better, not bitter. That's where I see so many people go wrong and I don't want that same result in my life. I want to move forward on my own and be stronger than I was before. I don't want my bounce back to make him jealous. I don't even want him checking for me. I want to live my life and let him live his life. I don't want any animosity. We have kids to raise. I want to co-parent from a pure place in my heart. I refuse to use my kids as chess pieces trying to play a game. I want to be whole and pure.

I want to encourage you to not let your pain keep you down. Don't be bitter. Don't be angry. It will hurt and you will feel every emotion, but don't stay there. Get up and keep going. Tell yourself over and over again the things you need to hear. Don't let anger settle in because that will keep you stagnant in your life. Be motivated to get better, to learn, and to grow. We only get one shot at this life so we can't waste too much time dwelling on the past and being stuck. Make a move.

CHAPTER 3

It's Not a Loss

We have to be careful what we consider a loss. If you learned from it then you didn't lose anything. I learned from my situation. I have to look myself in the mirror and I have to be real with myself. So I'm going to talk to myself and hope you get something from this. I'm not trying to be a life coach or a guru overnight, but I want to share with you the lessons I'm telling myself.

I first went wrong by not fully understanding what love looked like. I didn't take the time to learn love. I saw my parents have a successful marriage but I didn't take the time to get the real inside scoop on what I would face in a serious relationship. I just saw them have it and figured that I would figure it out and that it just comes. I'm a smart woman so I thought I'd figure it out just like my mom did. I wasn't prepared to love and I didn't know what I was doing. I didn't know what really makes a real man. I saw my dad but I didn't take the time to learn what made him who he is. I just thought that because I'm his daughter that I would attract a man like him who would marry me and love me for life. I made the mistake of comparing my life to my parents' life without really knowing everything my parents went through to build their relationship. That was a mistake that I believe most people make. They don't teach love in school and we don't sit down to learn about it at home either. We just live and expect things to fall into place, but that's not how it works.

The second mistake I made was getting caught up in the potential. I didn't weigh the facts. I wasn't thinking logically. He had this amazing heart and I could see so much goodness in him. I was not insecure and he hadn't giving me a reason not to trust him so I went with it. All in and so happy. He was already a big name when I met him and people would say that guys like that didn't want to commit.

I believed what he told me, which was that he was ready for it all — marriage, kids, and more. I was caught up in the timing of it all.

The third mistake I made was moving too fast. I had just come out of a relationship. I hadn't fully healed from my ex and then I meet this guy and I start to build without first being healed. If I had taken more time in between relationships then maybe I would have had a clearer mind and been able to notice game as it was being applied. I thought I was grown, but I was still growing in the relationship department. I jumped right into a relationship with him and we were basically living together rather quickly. I dropped what I was doing to be around him and we both were filling voids in each other. I think we were just convenient for one another. Obviously, we weren't meant to be now that I look back on it. But you could not have told me that at the time. All I knew was that he was who God handpicked just for me and I was grateful.

The fourth mistake I made was putting the cart before the horse. I should have never agreed to kids before a lifetime commitment. I gave him things he didn't deserve. You should only have the kids of your husband, but instead I was having the kids of a boyfriend, basically. I don't even believe in being engaged anymore because it doesn't count unless you're married. The laws don't protect fiancés. I love my kids and they are a huge blessing so I can't regret it now, but if I were to tell my kids anything about relationships it would be to build on real love and do things in the right order. Now my kids have to grow up in a co-parenting situation because their parents did things out of order. It's not the end of the world and they surely aren't the only ones growing up like that, but that doesn't mean it's right.

The fifth mistake I made was giving too much. I did things I knew I shouldn't have done. I gave of myself way too much. I compromised my self-respect trying to please my man. I was giving him so much but not getting much in return.

The sixth mistake I made was turning a blind eye. I became so wrapped up in the potential of the relationship and wanting it to work that I just put blinders on. I started to become more accepting and understanding of the cheating. I started to feel like cheating is normal and OK and at times I even condoned it. I began to lose hope in real love and I was settling for a mediocre love. I got complacent in that love.

The seventh mistake I made was staying in the relationship. I should have picked up and walked away when I had the chance. I ignored all the warning signs and all the disrespect thinking that he would come around. I was so desperate to keep my family together and to show him how dope I was. I knew I should have walked away. I got so comfortable in it all and the idea of a relationship that I ignored the fact that I didn't really have one at this point. I stayed long after I should have walked away.

I'm sure there are more mistakes I made that I could point out but I don't want this to be an encyclopedia. But I have to be honest about the things that I did wrong so I can learn from them. By doing this it helps me realize that it wasn't a loss, it was a lot of lessons. I actually gained because I have two beautiful kids and a lot of wisdom to move forward with. I can't look back and long for what I had. I have to look ahead to what's to come. If we lose love and we continuously look back on it as a loss then we'll never see what's in front of us. We have to realize that if we lost it, it wasn't meant to be. We have to gain lessons from mistakes instead of lamenting over them.

The mistakes become lessons and the people who were mistakes now become someone else's problem to deal with. All we can do is hope that our exes don't hurt anyone else the way they hurt us. If you wish bad on the next person then you're hindering your blessings. People have to grown on their own time, and unfortunately their growth may not happen with you. We have to be OK letting people go so they can grow.

So often we see couples break up and then move on to be extremely happy in their life in their next relationship. It's just the way that it happens when you love the wrong person and then you move on with a new sense of self and new lessons. We have to get over the fact that a relationship was only convenient and be OK that it wasn't meant to be.

Don't just go through life; grow through life. Take some time to sit and look over your last relationship and write down the lessons it taught you. Take those lessons and apply them to your life. Look at how it can benefit you in the future. I know now that the next man who comes into my life will have to come correct. He won't be able to get me to compromise my self-respect. He won't be able to lie and deceive. He won't be able to buy me or trap me. He will have to be ready to love and be ready for the love of a real woman.

The lessons can prepare you for your blessings. Once you learn everything that you don't deserve and then realize you can live through it, you're prepared to receive what you do deserve. You can see it like a practice run even though there may be some permanent things that came from it. You have to know that it's not your end but instead it's your beginning. Take the time to work on yourself and prepare for your next level.

One of the worst things we do is accept all the blame and guilt. I'm real about my situation and I realize what I did wrong but I can't blame myself for anyone else's mistakes and choices. I can't beat myself up for someone else's low self-esteem or lack of self-control. Those aren't my issues. I have to realize that I can only control so much. I can only control me. I can only take care of me. Yes, the choices of others can affect you but you can't live with the blame of it. You have to be able to look yourself in the mirror and speak into your life in a way that inspires you to keep pushing forward.

The funny thing about life is that when someone thought they were hurting you they don't realize that they were actually preparing you to receive even better. It's human nature sometimes to hope that the person you left behind never finds anyone better than you but you can't think like that. You can't wish that on them if you want to do better for yourself. It will work out in your favor and you will attract someone who is perfect for you. To your ex you're going to look so happy and it's going to show them that they weren't the one for you after all. Sometimes people want to look back at you just to see you still sitting where they left you. That's where you have to be strong enough and wise enough to get up and keep on moving. No one can stop you except you.

If you stand still hoping and waiting for someone to come back in your life you may be there waiting forever. That was my problem for maybe a little over a year. I was stuck. We were still living in the same house but not in the same bedroom. He was always gone for work, so it actually didn't feel any different to the kids. And maybe that's what made it so hard for me. I didn't do anything worth leaving over, so in the back of my mind I just knew that he would want to come back to his family. But very soon after, reality hit me and I had to snap out of it. In the end

I guess that it was easier for him to start over fresh with someone new rather that facing our issues and working through them. I thought about some advice that I gave a good girlfriend some time ago: If they left you then you have to assume that it's not meant to be. If they want you then they'll have to catch up with you down the road. Start hoping and praying for what's next. Start preparing for what's next. Let go of the past so you can open up for the future. There is nothing behind you worth going back to, but there is so much more ahead of you. We lose so much life and we miss so many blessings by looking back at what we once had. I'm thankful for the blessings and the lessons. If I could do it over there is very little that I would change because I had to go through those things to learn and to prepare myself for what's ahead of me. Everything happens for a reason and we have to understand that. It's not our will but it's God's will. Even when we step out of line we can still be under His grace, mercy, and protection. The moment you realize that is the moment that you start to find your strength to move forward with an open heart and an open mind. Love yourself and push yourself to the next level. There is no failure in life. There are tests and there are lessons. Get what's for you and let it make you a new person.

I'm praying for those who are stuck in a rut and can't seem to get out of it. It's my hope that you find your way and that your strength kicks in. I hope you can open your mind and form a new outlook on life and understand that everything will work out in your favor if you keep pressing. I hope that you will be able to realize your worth and not feel neglected, abandoned, or unworthy. I hope and pray that you'll find the strength where you feel like there is none. I hope that your dreams come true and you meet the love of your life and everything works out just fine.

It's all in our minds. Our thoughts will dictate our life. The way you look at your situation will determine how you handle it. Change the way you look at it and you will find yourself healing and growing much faster than you expected you would.

CHAPTER 4

Bigger Than Me

This hit me when I thought about my kids. There is so much that goes into this scenario but it starts with my kids. My kids are my world. I love them with all of my heart. I'm learning and growing as a mother every day. I've never claimed to be perfect or to be the best but I know I'm the best for them. I give my heart and my all to my kids and I can't let anything come before them. Of course it was a dream to have them raised in the home with their father. He was gone so much that it was like co-parenting anyways, but I realized there would come a time when he would be at home more and my kids would have their father on a daily basis. I wanted them to be able to run in the room and jump on top of him to wake him up. I wanted to see them wrestle around on the floor and see them team up on him. Those are the things all mothers dream of. No one dreams of being a single mother. No one dreams of co-parenting. No one dreams of another woman helping raise her kids. No one dreams of their kids calling another woman stepmom. That's not something that I thought was possible for my life. It's not something that I ever saw coming. But guess what? It came. And because it came I have to deal with it.

This is bigger than me because my kids are watching me. They are watching my every move. They had questions about daddy and when he was coming home. I lied to them for so long trying to keep hope alive. Then my heart was crushed the first time they told me about Daddy's new friend and they said her name. That's when it hit like a ton of bricks that I would have to get accustomed to my kids seeing another woman in the mother role on the weekends or whenever they are with their dad. Now I have to envision my kids climbing up in the bed with their dad and another woman. It hurts like crazy to process it but I know it's something I have to grow through. They need me. They need me to be strong and to be focused. They need me to get up every day and take life head on. If I lie down and quit that will send the wrong message to them. If I give up that will teach them to give up. If I flip out and go crazy on their dad that will drive a wedge between us. If I hold them hostage and keep them away from their dad that will hurt them because they love him dearly.

I have to get over myself and get out of my way for the sake of my kids. I have to be strong for them. It's up to me to be fair and to love. My kids need their father and want their father. Although he isn't in the home with them he is still in their life. So for them I have to forgive and forget. I have to get over my pain and move forward. They need to see me standing strong and living my life to the fullest. They can't see me down and out. I can't hurt them because I'm hurting. I see so many mothers get in the way of their children's development because they are mad with their child's father. It's not about the father anymore; it's about the kids. The kids need and want a good dad in their life and if you have a man in their life who treats them right then let him be there. Don't hold the kids hostage for more money or to get your way. Let them love their father and grow. The father will bring things to the table that you can't bring to the table. He will teach them lessons that you can't teach. So if you have a man who wants to be present and active, let him be there.

As women we have to accept that we went half on the baby. If he's childish, we slept with that childish man. If he's lame, we slept with that lame man. If he's a liar and a cheater, we slept with that liar and cheater. We have to realize that we are just as guilty as he is because we made a choice and with every choice there are consequences. I chose to have kids outside of wedlock and believe in a man's word. This is the price I'm paying. I have to live with that. The next time, I'll make sure a man gives me a lifetime commitment before I carry his child, if indeed I am able to reverse my permanent decision. We live and we learn. It's bigger than me.

There will come a time that I will have a man in my life. My husband might be reading this book and come looking for me. Guess what? My ex will have to deal with it. He will have to understand that my kids have a good man in the home with them every day and they will fall in love with him and see him as a second father. They will be fortunate enough to have two moms and two dads I guess you can say. That's the way life happens sometimes. At that point it will take a lot of maturity on both of our parts. We will have to be understanding and respectful.

It's my goal to harbor no bitterness whatsoever for the sake of our kids. I want to be able to go on vacations together if need be. There will be big moments in our kids' lives and we all will have to be there for them. We will have to be mature enough to do that. I already lost a relationship that never turned into marriage. I don't want to be one of those families that have to support the kids separately because we can't stand to be under the same roof at the same time. As long as his new person and my new person treat our kids with love and respect as if they were their own, I'll be OK. If that line is crossed then I will have some problems. I want my kids to be safe and to be educated about every area of life. I know one day I'll have to fully explain what happened. I'll have to explain to my daughter so that it doesn't happen to her and I'll have to explain to my son so he doesn't go through it either. I don't want to start something new with them. I don't want what happened to me to become a generational curse that's passed down from generation to generation. I will teach from my mistakes and urge them to save themselves for marriage or at least to not bring kids into the world before they have a real commitment. I know marriage isn't guaranteed to last but at least the attempt was made. You can't be mad at yourself if you do it the right way and it doesn't work out. But it's a whole different story when you do it your way and it doesn't work out.

Now that I'm in this situation it's about my kids being as stable and as normal as possible. It's new for me because I grew up in a two-parent home. That didn't make me perfect — I was a good kid but still a wild child at moments, Maybe this will strengthen my kids and help them be more cautious when they start dating.

Co-parenting isn't easy. We have to be real about the fact that we are sending our kids off to be with the other parent who is living their life and doing their thing. There may always be a little feeling there that we have to fight. Some people can fight the feeling and some people can't. It all comes down to how strong the bond was with your ex. With the fact that soul ties are real and very strong, it makes it hard to see the person you loved loving someone else. It will be hard for your kids to see their mother or father hugging and loving someone else. It's tough all the way around, but what matters most? The kids matter most.

Think about the perfect co-parenting scenario and it feels like an oxymoron because how can co-parenting be perfect? The act of co-parenting is painful in itself because a part of you wishes that it didn't have to be this way. Then when you get the tough questions from the kids that makes you want to crawl under the covers and never resurface. When you see their faces and you can see emptiness at times, it's heartbreaking. To fight through all of that, we have to make our best effort to make co-parenting as easy as possible. Nothing is easy in this life and co-parenting is definitely one of the hardest, especially if you have any pettiness in you. We have to admit that we can be petty at times. Being petty only hurts the kids in the end. Don't make your kids suffer just because you don't want to be strong enough to get over your feelings for their father.

Lord, help me fight the petty. I pray that I'm never put in the situation where the man doesn't want to provide for the kids financially. It's a tough situation for me because in my mind we were married, but on paper we were nothing. So when I was left high and dry, I didn't get half of anything. I had put my dreams on hold to support him and then I was left without a way to provide for myself because I'd given everything up. Fortunately he's being a good person and providing the roof and food so that as I'm building my brand and finding my way, our kids don't have to starve. I have a six-figure plan that I'm implementing, and it may even reach seven figures, but it takes time and I don't want my kids to lack anything in the process. I'm thankful that their father is there for them and providing for them. I pray I never have to see the day that he doesn't. There are a lot of situations we hear about when a woman wants a crazy amount of money per month in the man's mind and because of that he cuts them off and she ends up with no support, or they have to battle it out in court. Then sometimes the man doesn't want to deal with the courts and she knows that so she holds the kids hostage until he pays their ransom. I can't judge anyone's situation but I just hope and pray I never have to cross that bridge. That is when it becomes beneath us and we aren't thinking about the big picture.

The children matter the most. It's bigger than us. It's bigger than me. We have to find a common ground and think about the situation that will make the kids feel stable and comfortable. That is the main reason that I move how I move. Yes, some have said I'm crazy because he's worth so much that I should have taken him to court, but that's not what I'm about. I can make a way for myself. I am taking the steps to do so. And dragging their father to court, what kind of message is that sending to our kids? I trust that it doesn't bite me in the butt. I know that he will take care of his children. And when the kids are old enough to surf the internet — and they will — what they won't find is mommy acting a fool and keeping up mess.

We have to put our pain, anger, frustration, and other feelings aside. We have to focus on the well-being of the kids and what they need the most. Life is so much deeper than we think and if we can get out of our own way, things become so much easier. I'm working on me and starting to dig deeper to identify my "why." I want to lead by example for my kids and leave a legacy for them. It's something that I have to do. I'm not comfortable being taken care of by an ex-lover. I wasn't built like that.

I wrote my first childrens book a few years back when I was still in my relationship, and I'm almost done with the next two; one more for my daughter Madilyn and a first book for Mason. To see their faces when they tell me that they are proud of me is priceless. "My mommy wrote a book about me and my mommy is almost done writing a book about me." Oh my gosh! Nothing like it in the world and it makes me work even harder. I have to make it.

This book is another step, a bold one, toward independence and living my life on my terms. If you're in a situation like mine I urge you to find your way. Look inside of yourself and realize what's most important. Know that it's not about you anymore once you have kids. Now it's about the kids and their well-being. You can't depend on a man who is not your husband. You can't stand still and let life pass you by. If he's moved on you have to move on. Let your kids see your strength. Let them see you fight your way to the top. Lead by example and show them the way. Operate in class and dignity. Don't step out of character for a man. Don't stoop to his level if he's living beneath you. Stay classy and keep pressing your way.

Hard work always pays off. Work harder on yourself than you do on your job and you'll see a big difference start to happen. Don't get comfortable and don't get complacent. Push yourself to the next level and keep going no matter what's standing in your way. You can't slow down to watch what your ex is doing. You have to live your life and keep pressing. Let the world watch you. Let them see you win. Let them see you fight.

Always remember that it's bigger than you. It's up to you and it's on you because it's your life. Live it to the fullest and refuse to lose your way.

CHAPTER 5

Find Yourself

*A*s women we can get so caught up in a man that we neglect ourselves. I did just that. I want to be an actress, author, and business mogul. I was on that path when I met my ex. We met while we both were in the same city shooting movies. I was tapping into my gift and doing me. Then here comes a man and I got wide-eyed. I went from being wide-eyed to being pregnant, twice. After becoming a mom of two with a man who lives on the road it's very hard to have time for yourself. I was lost. My purpose became my kids and that's all that I did. Now I realize the importance of a complete balancing act. I wish I had stayed even just a little bit active in my dreams. They wouldn't have to be major, but just some movement in them would have put me in a better position. I was sleeping on my dreams. I should have been wide awake and pursuing them. I had the resources to make something happen but my focus was on home. There is nothing wrong with that but I got complacent as a girlfriend, fiancé, or whatever you want to call it. That burned me too. For some women it works out but it didn't for me so that's why I can't recommend that you drop everything for a man.

You have to find what you want to do in life and work toward it. We all have something we are good at and we have to tap into it. I'm working hard on myself and I'm stepping out on faith to make things happen. I did a reality TV show. I'm not a fan of reality TV shows but I wanted to give it a shot because I wanted to share myself with the world and show the world that all women who look like me don't act a certain way. Now you have my book and I plan to write others. Hopefully one day you'll see me in movies. You'll see events that I produce, you'll see me at events inspiring women, and so much more. It's time to find me. It's time to follow my dreams and live my life. I'm not under a man now so I can be free to pursue the things that I enjoy. I have to create something or else I'll be wasting away in this life.

Think about your gifts and what you'd like to do with your life. Make a plan and then take action. Don't be afraid to fail. No matter what you want to do there is always a way to do it. The book you're reading I decided to take into my own hands. I wanted to make it happen on my own. I didn't want to go begging publishers to publish my book so I said I'll do it through my own publishing company, the one that I started when I wrote my childrens book in 2013. I didn't want someone telling me what I could and couldn't say in the book so I got with my people and we made it happen. That's the space that I believe we have to operate from. We have to have a make-it-happen attitude in order to succeed in life. As you've heard said before, nothing comes to a sleeper but a dream. There isn't anything that you're serious about that you can't bring into fruition. You have to know that and be willing to work for it.

What I've noticed is that a lot of men want to sit a woman down. It's happened since the beginning of time so it's nothing new, I'd say. I remember around the time that we first broke up was our family vacation time. Some people didn't want me to go but it was my son's first time going out of the country and I wasn't missing that for the world. I was also thinking that my ex would see his family unit and realize that he didn't want to break up this beautiful home after all. But oh was I ever wrong. After the kids were asleep he came to my room because we needed to talk. I was at my lowest. I cried, asked if he wanted to go to counseling. I tried it all. I didn't want any of this for our kids or myself. That very night he told me that I have this amazing light that shines and he would only be holding me back if he came back. I have always been told that since I was a kid, but he had never said that to me. It could have been one of his excuses because now in his new relationship he is doing the exact opposite of everything he did in our relationship. Nevertheless I went on to tell him that I wanted my family. I said I would stay home with the kids if that was what he wanted again. I was willing to throw away all of my dreams forever but little did I know that my God had a plan. He wanted so much more for me. The pain that I was feeling at that moment was so bad and I didn't understand it at all but I get it now. So I want to thank him right now because I never did. Thanks for not listening to me and not letting me waste away my talents and my dreams. Yes, some men want to sit you down and have you focus on him and the kids only. There is nothing wrong with that if the man is going to protect and provide for you until death do you part. But in this day and age that's not even promised. And if he's cheating, lying, and misleading you then you have to see that early and make some changes. You have to start lining things up for yourself and getting out there and making things happen. You can't get stuck in the world doing only what a no-good man wants you to do. A man who doesn't have the best intentions for you will sit you down so that you feel like you need him forever. He will try to isolate you so that you depend only on him. Beware of that and don't let it happen. If you work on you then you'll have something to fall back on if he decides that he wants something new one day. I made the mistake and I don't want you to make that mistake.

Get in your zone. Start thinking about what you do well and start doing it. There are many women becoming millionaires online today. Women earning major bucks right through Instagram and

Youtube. There is so much opportunity today that it's scary almost. It's time that we tap into our gifts and start making things happen. I refuse to be in the same place next year. I'm college educated, I have a degree in psychology. I want to make a lot of my own money and be my own person. My eyes are open for my opportunities and I'm working on myself so that I'm prepared for the opportunity when it comes. I'm more than capable. I had to ask myself, "What am I good at?" It's a question that can baffle you if you've spent so much time catering to others. But it's a question we have to confront and find the answer to. When you're honest with yourself you'll realize that there is so much that you can do if you put your mind to it. We just don't oftentimes because we fear failure.

It's time to step out on faith and make some things happen. Hang with people who have dreams and goals. It's cool to relax and have a good time but it should be after you've had a long, hard week of work. You can't relax too much or you'll miss your opportunities. There is always something that you can be doing.

One of the things I'm working on and I want to encourage you to do as well is a nonprofit organization. I think at the foundation of it all we should be givers. If you can't identify any other gift there is one thing you can do and that's help others. You can serve where you suffered. For me, I'm going to help children being raised in a single-parent home. I'm going to help men and women who are starting over after a bad breakup. I'm going to help domestic violence survivors and people who were left broken. I didn't go through all of those things but my heart can relate and I know what it feels like to be hurt and have to start all over. I want to help those people.

I already help a few nonprofits. A couple of years back I took care of 48 kids in Swaziland, Africa for an entire year. I also visited the country on a life-changing mission trip. I told my friend about it and she dropped everything and came along for the ride. She also started matching what I was giving to help the families there. I was blown away. After that trip we were not the same. It is so important to have great friends who are there for you, but I will touch more on that later. I cannot wait to go back to Africa. With my funds they built an orphanage that was named after my company, which is named after my kids, The Evan Grace Angel House Orphanage.

My son's name is Mason Evan and my daughter's name is Madilyn Grace. It is super important for me to teach them the importance of giving back even at this young age. A lot of people don't realize that a nonprofit organization doesn't mean that you're just giving away all of your money. It's an actual business that you can run and also make a living while living your purpose and serving others. Those are the types of things that interest me even more so now.

I'm taking time out for Monyetta. I have to reconnect with myself and find what I want to do and what makes me come alive. It's not an easy thing to do but it must be done. I don't have a choice but to do it. It's sad that sometimes we don't do what we need to do until we have to do it. But I guess it's better late than never.

It's time to carve out some time for you. It's time to force the situation and find a way to do what you love to do. It will not be easy; I'm learning that now but I know it will be worth it. We sit back and watch other people live so much that we fail to live our lives. We have to stop watching other people live and start helping ourselves.

My prayer is that I never lose my identity in a man again. My prayer is that I can love me as much as I love my neighbor and that I can make myself a priority. I believe that if we can find ourselves we can live a much happier life. But as long as we depend on someone else to make us happy we will always be at their mercy. They can make us and they can break us and that's not the type of power I want to give away anymore.

I've been taught recently that a relationship should consist of two independent people who are mature enough to be interdependent. It's interesting when you think about it because a lot of relationships have one independent person and the other person becomes a dependent. What we have to realize is that a dependent is a child or a special needs person. If you're not a child or a special needs person then you shouldn't be depending on anyone else. You have to find your own way.

I think the days are over of women playing the background, and we have to be OK being the bread-winner, and we have to force a man to respect us as such. There are more and more power moves being made my women in this world and we can't be afraid to join the ranks. Yes, there are many men who are intimidated by a woman on her grind but we have to be on our grind. A real man will see your worth and respect your hustle. He won't try to stop you from doing your thing. He will support you in every way possible. That man may be rare but rare women attract rare men.

Sit down after reading this book and start going over your success plan. Share your plan with a trusted friend who you know will support you. Speak your plan into existence and set out to take action. Don't waste anymore time living beneath your talent level. If you are already on your grind then take it up a notch. Surprise yourself. There won't only be one Oprah in this lifetime. Someone else has to help change the world so it should be one of us.

I'm trusting that women can step up in major ways and love ourselves inside and out. We've been put down and run over for so long that it comes a time that we have to demand the respect that we expect. Respect is rarely given; it's earned. If you want to be taken seriously then you'll have to take yourself more seriously. It's great to work for someone else but it's even better to have something you can call your own. And it's OK to do both. I've been told over and over that real men are attracted to ambitious women. You may have to focus on the kids like me but you can work behind the scenes at the same time and keep making moves for yourself along the way. There are no limits other than the limits you place on yourself. We have to get out of the woman-box and start thinking bigger than what society has placed on us. I'm tired of being a glorified piece of arm candy who has to depend on a man who isn't my husband. I'll sit down for my husband if our lifestyle calls for it but never again will I sit down for anything less than that.

A lot of times men will tell us that they never told us to sit down, but we felt it. We knew that if we worked for what we wanted the same way they did then our kids would never see us. So we bite the bullet and we carry the load. We become the CEO at home and we keep everything running smoothly. It's a tough balancing act but I believe we are very capable of doing more than one thing at a time.

Don't let life pass you by while you're supporting the dreams of others. Make sure you take the time to support your own dreams as well. We have no other choice but to love ourselves. Life is too short to waste it living beneath our potential.

CHAPTER 6

Mind, Body, And Spirit

*I*t's great to build business and use our gifts but I've come to realize that we have to focus on the inside too. After my breakup I started working on my mind first. I had to get new knowledge. I had to grow to understand what I did wrong and what he did wrong. I wanted to learn more about love and how we get it confused with other things that have nothing to do with love. I had to start reading books, listening to teachings online, having countless conversations with my spiritual advisor, my pastor, and my father, going to seminars, working with a life coach, going to church more, and really feeding my mind. I had to learn the things that I'd never learned. There was no class at any level of school that was called "Love 101" or "Life 101." I had to really sit and learn so that I could identify my mistakes and move forward with my life in a more healthy way. I'd done some things in my past relationship that I had no clue were wrong. In my learning process I realized that I compromised my self-respect in ways that I couldn't recover from in that relationship. I belittled myself and truthfully I lost the respect in my relationship. I had no clue what I was doing was wrong. I thought I was pleasing my man and being the woman he needed me to be. I gave too much. I disrespected myself. I turned a blind eye and paid the price. I needed more knowledge, wisdom, and understanding, and that's what I set out to do. I've been getting knowledge and I'm still doing so. It's a process. It's something that we have to do daily. I try my best to learn something new every day. They say knowledge is power and I want to be powerful. If I had known that some of the things I was allowing to happen in my home could cost me my relationship I wouldn't have done them. But that's what happens when we don't know any better. I had to learn the hard way and because of that I'm trying to help others.

While I'm getting knowledge about life, love, and myself I also have to watch what I allow to enter my mind. When feeding your mind you have to protect your mind. You have to guard your mind from things that will lead you astray. I had to cut back on junk TV, junk music, and junk conversation. I have to protect my mind and filter what enters it. It's amazing how what we watch and what we listen to can influence us so much. We don't realize it most often but it shapes our views on everything in life. I had to take control of my mind and stop allowing myself to be polluted with junk. We can only produce from what's inside of us so I had to change what was going in my mind. There is so much drama and negativity in our world that if we aren't careful we can be consumed by it and it can destroy us slowly. I didn't want that to happen to me so I took it upon myself to start changing my thoughts and enlightening myself so that I could produce more in life.

The mind is a terrible thing to waste but so is the body. Every body is different but it's all we have to live in so we have to treat it right. It's been my focus while I'm healing to do right by my body. I realize that what I put into my body will determine my lifetime and I want to live a long time. As women we go through so much with having kids, mini depressions, ups and downs with the stress of relationships, and so on. It gets very hard to take care of your body when you have so much else on your mind. I'm still a work in progress. Being a Louisiana girl I love to eat. Food is everything to me. The food I eat can be unhealthy at times but I've been conscious about it and working on it for years now. I want to eat right and live right. They say abs are made in the kitchen and I want me some abs so I'm doing my best to take care of my body. The funny thing about bodies is that we are told that it has to be a certain way. My booty may be a little too big for my waist. My thighs may be too thick. My breasts may be too small (changed that over ten years ago). But guess what? I have to love me the way that at I am. If I can't fix it in the gym or by the way I eat then I have to control over it. I'm learning to love every curve, all the cellulite, and every blemish. My body is my temple and I have to love me for who I am.

I want you to think about the pressure you put on yourself to look a certain way. Why do we do it? We do it to please a man and impress other women. We have to realize that God made us all different and the person for you will like your natural shape. Don't kill yourself trying to be a certain size. Don't kill yourself trying to alter your body in every way possible. Bust your butt in the gym and eat right. Then let the rest fall into place. You're unique and you have to be OK with that. I can no longer try to please the world and lose myself in the process. Every part of my life must be in line with my ultimate goals. It's time to focus on me and work diligently on me.

Another part of my life that I'm focused on is my spirit. From your spirit flows everything in your life. You have to be centered to produce at your highest level. If you're drained spiritually and your spirit becomes very toxic as a result then you're losing the battle. While working on my spirit I started to focus on specific areas. I wanted to gain peace. Peace is very necessary to be a good parent and a good person. I wanted peace in my heart and mind so I worked toward it by controlling my actions. I was able to shake free from a lot of spirits by cutting certain TV shows and other things I was allowing in my life. I love God and I'm working on my relationship with Him daily. I was raised in the church and I'm a Christian who isn't perfect.

I've made so many mistakes and done things I'm not proud of, but I know that I serve a loving and forgiving God. I'm living in His grace and mercy every day. I've had to cleanse and purify my spirit over the last year. When you allow yourself to get bogged down in a toxic relationship you start to lose yourself. You can lose your peace, joy, and happiness. You have to get centered and start to pour into your spirit so you can grow and experience the joy and happiness you were intended to. It's a battle and a lot of times we don't understand when we are under attack. We overlook the fact that what we are going through isn't just physical but it's spiritual. Spiritual warfare is very real and it can destroy you from the inside out. You have to take care of your inner man and guard your spirit from those toxic spirits that will strip you. I was in a spiritual warfare and I was losing the battle. I was giving into spirits that were beneath me and they derailed me from my purpose for some time. I'm almost back to myself now. I've been working more and more on myself and not giving into the negative energy that seems to surround me so often. I can't lose myself again. I have to fight and I have to win at any cost. My kids need me. They feed off of my energy. If I'm sad it makes them sad. If I'm down it makes them down. I have to stay spiritually fed so they can feed off of me. Everything flows from there. We have to be sure that we don't take on the spirits of the people we are around. I'm sure you've heard it said that you're a make-up of the five people you spend the most time with. If that's true then you have to be very careful who you let around you. I've grown more conscious of my surrounding and my circle of influence. Misery loves company, as they say. I don't want to be miserable on the account of someone else. I need to stand on my own two feet and dictate my destiny by living in peace the way I want to.

I really want you to sit and think about the things you need to work on. I know it has been such a blessing for me. If you can focus in on the things in your life that need changing and then be committed to the change you will be surprised by what can happen. We have to work harder on ourselves. We are living in a lazy society today and so many people want microwave success, microwave bodies, and microwave love. We risk so much trying to get it the easy way. I want to go about it differently. I want to make changes that will last and take me to the next level in life. I want to vibrate on a higher level and attract those people on that level into my life. I can no longer live on a low-frequency vibration and expect to get massive results.

I urge you to buy in as well. It's time that we stop being victims and start being victors. We have to build ourselves up and stop depending on someone else to build us up. If it's meant to be, it's up to me. I heard that quote in grade school and I'll never forget it. Another quote that resonates with me is one that my middle school principal Albert Hardison (a great man) used to say at every school program. It was and still is the motto at Walnut Hill Elementary and Middle School. "Work for the best. Accept only the best. Be the very, very best." And that is exactly what I am doing. It's time out for living on someone else's terms and living on their timeline. I'm reworking my plan and I'm making it happen. Failure is no longer suitable for me. I have to succeed and I have to win from the inside out. I want to be a whole person. I don't want to be empty on the inside and going around the world pretending to be whole. It's time we wake up and stop playing games with ourselves. So many people will doubt you and put you down but you have to make up your mind that you're going to fix your life. You have to make up your mind that your mind, body, and spirit will be in pristine condition and that you will excel in this life. Be very careful what you settle for.

Don't let a man tie your spirit down with his twisted soul tie. Men realize they have power over us once they enter us. Once we have sex we take things to another level. We give away a piece of our spirit and a man knows how to manipulate us with that piece that we give away. Take your time and make sure that you build a real relationship. Make sure you have a real man in your life who loves and respects you. You are not a sex slave. You are not a sex toy. You are fearfully and wonderfully made. You have to know that and you have to believe that. If you don't guard your spirit then you will be taken for granted. You will be used up and then left to rot. Take my word for it. I went through it. You have to get to the place in your life where you require a man to work extremely hard for your heart. It's not that you want to play games. It's that you don't want him to play games with you. You have to have standards and guard yourself from the tricks of the world. So many people are so spiritually void that if they can bankrupt your spirit they will do exactly that! We give so much and we get so little in return. We crawl on the floor trying to keep a man from leaving. We worship him as if he's God and we put God on the back burner. We start to depend on that man instead of depending on our creator. That's what I'm coming to realize and that's what I'm growing through. No more lies. No more games. No more men who don't love me for me. I'd rather be single than to have a man in my life who doesn't respect my mind, body, and spirit.

Gather yourself. Make your plan. Renew yourself. You don't have to settle and you don't have to suffer!

CHAPTER 7

I Forgive You

I forgive you. I gave my heart. I gave my mind. I gave my everything. I believed in you. I believed in every word you said. I held onto your words as if they were gospel. I trusted you with my life. I allowed you to convince me that I would be safe and that you'd love me until the end of time. I knew that you would forever be mine. I put myself through so much trying to please you. I did things for you that I'll regret for the rest of my life. I gave too much. I didn't know that I was being lied to. I didn't know that I was just a temporary love. I didn't know that my attempt to "go hard" for my man was only sabotaging myself. I didn't know that the lust would run out and I'd be left to realize that you never were really in love with me. I apologize for getting complacent if that's what it was. I apologize for living off of you if that was never your intention. If I'm to blame, I apologize for that too. I had no clue because I just loved you.

I never in a million years would have thought that I'd be replaced by another woman. I never fathomed the possibility of my children calling another woman stepmother. I never thought that I'd have to share my two beautiful angels. I had those angels for you, for us. I had those angels thinking that's what we both wanted. Remember, "Let's go get forever," wasn't that how you used to say it? I thought they were the icing on the cake. I never thought they would be the only ones loving me. I thought that you were my world and that I was your world. I believed that the laughs, the smiles, and the late-night conversations were all real. Now I know that it wasn't real. It was all to pass time. I was a good fling that came with some permanent things, like two children. I was an egg donor to a man who wanted to sow his seeds. I guess I'll have to be that.

I don't want you to think that this is a guilt trip. I don't want you to think that I feel sorry for myself. I'm just writing from my heart and saying what most people in my position are afraid to say. I don't blame myself although you may blame me. I'm not angry anymore. I'm not bitter. I'm not sure when all of the pain will go away but I'm getting stronger every day. A part of me will always love you because the love from me was real. Real love doesn't just get up and walk away. I have to love you because I see your face every day. Every time I look in their eyes I see you. I'll be OK and I'll love you from a distance. I'll root you on and wish you the best. I want you to be happy. I want you to be at your best because our children need you at your best. I won't wish anything bad on you. I won't hold it over your head. I won't be mad at your new love. She's an innocent bystander and I just hope she never has to feel the pain I've had to feel. I didn't know it would ever get this real. I thought the love was real but now I realize that the pain is greater. I won't walk away believing that love is pain. I'll let this experience make me stronger. I'll teach our kids from my mistakes with the hopes that they won't repeat them. I don't want you to feel sorry for me.

I don't want you to come running back. We ran our race. I'd have to say you won but I don't really feel that way. I won because I'm still standing. My victory doesn't mean that it's your defeat. It means that I won't beat myself up anymore over what I've lost. I've moved on and I'm staying strong. I will continue to lift up our kids and make sure they are strong. I'll be a rock for them and for myself.

I wouldn't wish this pain on my worst enemy. The pain and embarrassment will one day completely fade away I know. But for now I'll embrace the struggle because I can feel it making me stronger. I have to keep pressing. I have to keep fighting. It's interesting to see how this love turned out. I don't think anyone who knew me expected that this would become my story. I guess I have to wear this crown with my head held high. It happened to me so I'd assume it could happen to anyone. I'm looking for all of the lessons in the loss. I see them and I feel them but sometimes it's still hard to admit them. I'm not sure if you know what it feels like to have your love walk out on you and truthfully I hope you never have to. It's not something I'd ever want to see you go through.

I'm writing this open letter because I'll never give this to you. I'm not doing it for me, honestly, I'm doing it for everyone who needs to forgive someone who has hurt them. Forgiveness can be such a hard thing to do but it's a necessary thing to do. I know that I can't truly move forward unless I forgive you. I heard it said before that forgiveness is a gift you give yourself. Well, I guess I'm treating myself today. My biggest hope is that this letter is a treat for someone else too. If I've hurt you I hope that you can find it in your heart to forgive me as well. Our kids will need to see that we still have some love, even if it's just a love for them. I hope that this breakup doesn't break our hearts for good. I hope that we both can truly love again. You seem to be doing just fine but I'm all too familiar with the many masks we can wear. I'm hoping that the smile on your face isn't one of a clown and that beneath it there's not a frown. I'm slowing finding my smile again and I know one day I'll meet someone who can appreciate it for what it truly is. I want to truly be happy again and I know happiness is a choice. I'm choosing right now to be happy with the way things have turned out. I can't sit and sulk and cry anymore. I have to forgive and forget. They say that it's easier said than done and I can finally say that I understand what they mean by that. I'm saying it but I hope I can continue to do it. I'm a work in progress every day. Many times we don't like to be vulnerable but I realize it's necessary for growth. We have to be able to come to this point to find our true strength. I am wishing you the best on your journey!

I hope that letter will help you see the power in forgiveness. I'd like for you to write your own letter too. It doesn't have to be a poem and it doesn't have to be long. I am sure there is someone you need to forgive and what better to do than to write a letter. You may never get a chance to give it to them but writing it can help you heal. Not forgiving will only hurt you. The person you need to forgive will move on with their life and they may even forget how bad they hurt you, but if you hold onto the resentment you'll never heal. Find it in your heart to forgive because the same forgiveness that you grant to someone else will be the forgiveness you need granted to you one day. I hope you can take that step to open up and let forgiveness in. It's too painful to carry hate, anger, bitterness, and resentment. We have to find a way to give it to God and let him take away the pain. Forgiving makes you the bigger person. It clears your path ahead so that you can move forward without having to forever look behind you. You can let go and free yourself up to receive what's next. Forgiveness is so very necessary.

Never give anyone the satisfaction of knowing that you can't get over them. You have to walk in your strength and let them know that although they may have knocked you down, you won't stay down. When they see you get up they will realize that you're stronger than they thought and they will realize that they took a good heart for granted. Losing you is their loss. Hurting you is their loss. But if you don't forgive then it's your loss. I understand forgiveness on a whole different level now. I've had to forgive for things I just never thought I'd have to forgive someone for. I went through things that could have broken me down for good.

I can't put everything that went on in the relationship in this book. I believe in being transparent but I also believe that some things are just your business. I'm not a tell-all type of woman and it's not my wish to hurt my ex or myself. I don't want to tarnish either of our names. We have kids to raise and I have to be cognizant of that fact. There are things

that I will never forget. Things that have happened
that make it hard to forgive but I want to let it go.
I want to move forward. You may find yourself in
a situation one day where you give everything. You
may make life-altering decisions for your partner
and things still not work out like you had envisioned
but you still have to move forward. In the heat of
the moment we do things in relationships that we
may regret for a lifetime. We make permanent decisions sometimes based on temporary emotions.
Those decisions can later play a part in our need
to forgive someone for what happened in our lives.
I don't believe that people are malicious at heart. I
think sometimes we act out of ignorance and fear.
We do things to a person or ask things of a person
from a selfish place and we don't think about the
consequences. Life isn't always crystal clear when
you're in a relationship and trying to find your way.
It's easy for someone to hurt you while trying to
find their way. There will always be an opportunity
to get hurt while trying to love. You have to love
as if you haven't loved before and you can't hold
back because you fear being hurt. If you fear being
hurt then you will for sure get hurt at some point.
If you're going to be in it then be in it. Give your

all and let the chips fall where they may. Love is a gamble that we all take at some point. Sometimes we win and sometimes we lose, but I believe that the effort is worth the risk. As they say, it's better to have loved and lost than to have never loved at all.

I can't live with hate in my heart. I can't dwell on the past to the point that it cripples me from moving toward my destiny. I've gone through some things for love that I can't ever change. I put my heart on the line. I put my life and dignity on the line. I gave up a huge part of me trying to please a man. Forgiveness is not easy for me but it's necessary. I know there may be some things that you've gone through that are far worse than what I went through, but even still you have to find forgiveness in your heart. Forgiveness is not just for them; it's for you.

I urge you to free yourself from the bitterness you're harboring and to let it go and move forward in your life.

CHAPTER 8

Will I Find Real Love?

I think this is a question that so many women
have. I sure have that question more than ever now.
I've always been in a relationship, but oh how things
change when you start getting up in age and kids are
in the picture. You start to wonder who is going to
love you now? It can get scary sometimes and then
there are times that I feel desperation setting in and
I have to cancel it out very quickly. I'm at a point in
my life where I'm wondering what type of man is
the man for me. I'm wondering if there is real love
still left in our cold world. I know deep down that
I believe it will happen but as a human I entertain

the thoughts sometimes, maybe just like you do. Are there any real men left? I know real men but they all seem to be happily in love. Are there any real men still looking for love or are there just too many women to go around? It gets hard at times when you really think about it. In my mind I'm a great woman, but I don't know how men view me. I have to be careful not to let what happened to me affect the way I view myself. One man had me have two kids and then left me, then shortly after married another woman. If I let it that could ruin me going forward so I have to fight that perception. For me it's tougher because it will take a special man to love a woman whose ex is famous. My new man will have to hear and see my ex on TV and the radio. I'll need a man who is strong and secure in who he is. I'll need a man who knows that my ex wasn't the man for me and that I'm still in need of that real man in my life. That may not be easy to find but I know it will come.

As women we have this clock ticking so we think. We feel the pressure from society to be married. We feel the pressure from parents and friends at times. We struggle with the timelines that others have put on us, and the ones that we've put on ourselves. It's not easy to balance your wants and your needs. The pressure of society can get pretty heavy when you start to look up and realize you'll be 40 soon and you still aren't married. It seems like we are in a society of fiancés. I see a record number of engagements but so many of them never turn into a marriage. Then when you do see a marriage, so many of them end in divorce. It can make you wonder if this is something you really want to go through with. Even with all of that around me I still want my shot at real love. I want the opportunity to love my husband until death do us part. Like my parents still have to this very day. I want that real love. Last time I had something else but it wasn't 100% real. I got two beautiful kids out of it but it didn't last so I'm still longing for something real, something to call my own.

It's tough to see women who I don't think match up to me get married. I ask myself, *What am I doing wrong? Am I not showing enough skin? Do I need to learn how to work the pole? Is the food I cook not tasty enough? What's wrong with me?* Nothing is wrong with me. What is wrong is this society. We live in a society of men who have forgotten what it is to be a man. They want their cake to sit and look pretty on the countertop but they also want a cake they can eat too. You can't have both but they seem to want both. They want a superwoman who has a perfect body, cooks, cleans, is ambitious, slides down a pole, has amazing sex and naughty habits, but yet can still be a good mom and shine in a boardroom. They want a woman that is above and beyond what they are as a man. There are women who can pretend to be all that a man dreams of but that act will get old fast. That man will realize that he's been duped and then will be stuck. What happens to the women who are real? The women who learn themselves and fall in love with themselves? Where do we fit in? Will we be forever overlooked? Will we be back in style again? Will we be just a convenient love for a period of time and then left for someone younger and hotter? We need real love to come back. Do you remember that love that lasted a lifetime? That love where the couple still held hands at 70? I want that type of love to come back. We have this microwave love today. The love where a man asks a woman to marry him but it's only to #WasteHerTime2016, or whatever the year may be. We have the love where the man wants her to be OK with him cheating and running the streets in real life. The one that doesn't question anything. I'm not into that type of love. I tried it but it wasn't me. I want more than that.

What are we to do in a world with this type of love? As women we have to know who we are. We have to know what we want. We have to know what we're worth. We have to have standards that we are unwilling to compromise. We have to be bigger than ourselves. We can't be desperate. We can't give in and start trying to fit into society like I once did. We can't lose our class. We can't drop our guards and start to cave in because we are so desperate to be a man's wife. I know there will come a time for us all. It's my hope that the tide will turn and real men will come back in style, and those men will seek out real women. If we want it to change then as women we have to change it. As long as we are willing to just lie on our backs and be treated like floor mats then that's exactly how men will treat us. We can't expect a man to just give us respect if we don't demand it. You don't get what you're worth in life. You get what you negotiate. A person will treat you exactly how you allow them to treat you. We have to understand that and be willing to demand what we want. I don't believe men are bad at their core. I believe society has gone down and men have gotten lazy. I believe there have been so many passes given to men that they expect a pass now. But deep down I believe a man can elevate to the call if he is forced to. If a man if forced to respect you because you won't settle for anything less, then I believe he is capable of doing just that. If we let men have their way then they will have their way. You can't lie down for sex on the first night and expect a horny man to say, *No, get up you deserve better than this.* In a perfect world that would be great but we don't live in a perfect world. We live in a real world and we have to protect ourselves first before we expect a man to protect us. Humans are selfish by nature because everyone wants to survive. So therefore if a man sees that you're going to let him live off of you he will do that. He may only do what he has to do, not what you want him to do. I've learned the hard way. The sad part is that as women sometimes we learn the same lessons about men over and over again. I don't know about you but I'm tired of learning the same lessons over and over. It's time for change. It's time for something new to take place in my love life. I'm confident that it can happen but I know it will take time.

We have to identify exactly what type of man we want in our lives. Then be present-minded and open to attracting that man. I will need a man who is mature enough to hold a great conversation with me. I will need a man who is mature enough to love my kids as his own. I will need a man who is financially stable and ambitious in his pursuit of better. I need a man who loves God and wants to live that lifestyle of a real Christian. I need a man who is confident and knows who he is and doesn't let other men intimidate him.

I'm guessing the list could go on but I'm coming to realize that we have to be firm in what we want but yet realistic at the same time. I don't want a list as long as a book because I'll never meet that man. I don't want to ask a man to bring more to the table that I'm bringing. We may not bring it in the same ways but I want to be an equal contributor in the relationship. I'm opening up for love because I notice that it's so easy to overlook good men. A lot of good men are introverts and their attempts to get your attention are different than the player type. I'm working on being more present and paying attention to my surroundings. I'm no longer shooting a man down in one second. I'm open to conversation and a man shooting his shot. After his shot is out there then I can decide to accept it or turn it down, but I'm changing the way I approach dating. We live in a totally new world so we have to be open to meeting a man online, on social media, through matchmaking, or a plethora of other ways. Love can be looking you in the face every day but if you're too focused on your pain, your past, or moving too fast you'll miss it.

You can't move into your next relationship and get too caught up comparing your next to your ex. You have to wipe the slate clean and start over fresh. We talked about forgiveness. Well forgiveness should be what gives you the strength to start over and to love brand new. You have to give a man a fresh start in your life. Give him the opportunity to prove himself to you. If you let him in but he already has two strikes against him in your mind, it won't last very long. It's not fair to a man to have to pay for the mistakes your ex made. Let your past lessons make you confident, not bitter. Let the lessons prepare you for real love, not cripple you from love. I always hear men complaining about bitter women. I know there are bitter men too. But who is to blame? We are all human and I know it's natural to have your guards up really high and tight after being hurt. It's common sense. But we have to have our guards up without it showing in our face, conversation, and body language. We have to be aware of the games and looking for them but not let it make us block what could be a blessing.

Have you ever run a good man off? That's what we have to be careful of. A man won't work for too long if he feels like his work is in vain. A man can tell when your heart is still with another man. So if you say you want real love then you have to prepare to receive it. You have to truly be open to receive it. As you know, love will come when you least expect it. I know I'm getting ready for it now. I'm finally at the place where I am dating and ready to receive the love that I desire. I don't think we can ever be 100% ready, and we will always have to grow with our partner, but it would be wise to at least be as whole of a person as possible. If you're incomplete or empty then love won't fill you up. You will pull something different out of your partner if you're empty. Your partner may see you as a pushover and have the urge to fully deplete you and run over you instead of filling you up. It's sad that we attract what we are but there is truth to it. In a perfect world we would meet a prince charming who comes in and fills every void and makes us whole, but it's not how it works. As I've been taught, a mate complements you, not completes you.

CHAPTER 9

Brand You!

We are all a brand and it's important that we act like one. I remember when I gave up my brand and I settled for just being a girlfriend to a man. I forgot who I was and I was living in the shadows. I refuse to live that way again. It's time to build business. It's time for women to start seeing ourselves differently in the marketplace and to start dreaming out of the box.

I'm learning that there is so much power in being a brand instead of just being a person. We get so comfortable living off of someone or working for someone that we fail to create something for ourselves. I'm starting to realize that I am a company. I am the CEO of my life. I need to have a board. I need to have policies and procedures. I need to have a mission statement and I need to hire and fire people from my life. I have to change the way I see myself and the way I operate.

I've even heard a man say that men may choose a less attractive woman over an attractive woman because the less attractive woman has a brand. How does that work? I believe that what it says about you when you take control of your life is that you're capable of taking charge in the home and being the CEO of a home too. If you can get out and start something for yourself then you can maintain a household. Branding yourself adds to your sexy.

Go out and start your company. It doesn't have to be big and it doesn't have to earn millions of dollars. Even if it's just a blog or an online store, have something that you own. Take out time for yourself. Work with a life coach, business coach, or mentor. Find what it is you like and build it relentlessly. You have to maximize this life and make your dreams a reality. I think we let people tell us what we can't do too often.

As a brand you will carry yourself differently because once you start your own thing you have too much to lose. Now it's bigger than you. Now sleeping with a man comes with too many repercussions if you have something to lose. Now merging your company with someone who isn't doing anything in their life just doesn't look appealing. There are a lot of sad excuses for men who will come in your life and try to take over what you've built but when you sweat over something you won't turn it over as easy. We have to see ourselves like a brand even when we don't have a company or a hustle about us. That's why it is so important that we carry ourselves in a certain manner. The world is always watching your brand. You must be aware of what you are putting out there. Make sure whatever you do is done with class.

CHAPTER 10

Choose Your Circle Wisely

My circle is small. I have friends and then I have associates. I'm not the type to keep my enemies close. Having a tight circle is what really helped me get through the trying times. It was my friends who were there when things were good and there when things were bad. They weren't fair-weather friends. They didn't just come around to see my misery; they celebrated the good times with me as well. I don't know what I would have done if it wasn't for my friends and my loved ones. It's a beautiful feeling when your family is also your friends. In a world of fake friends it's important that we have people around who genuinely care. My friends and family have been my rock while I was getting over my breakup and building my company and brand. It hasn't been easy but having people there for me who care has really helped me a lot.

In your circle you need different types of people. You need someone for each role. You have to have people around you who bring something to the table. You can't have freeloaders and leeches and call them friends. Your friends should add to your life not subtract. It's hard to find good people so if you have some don't let them go. When you least expect it your friends will save the day in ways you never imagined. When you can't sleep at night and all you can do is cry you need that friend who will listen to you, cry with you, and pray with you. When you need to brainstorm for a business move you need that friend who can give you great ideas and encourage you in every endeavor. When you need a dose of reality and you want to hear the truth you need that friend who will keep it real with you and not sugarcoat the truth. And I am fortunate enough to also have my dad for that. He keeps it so real, never sugarcoats, and always has a scripture and a word to back up what he says. When you're feeling down and need a pick-me-up you need that person who can encourage you and speak into your life in a way that makes you want to get up and make something happen. When you want to kick back and have fun you need that friend who knows how to have a good time. You need good people around you and you have to give what you want to receive.

I look around and I see so many people with fake friends. It hurts to see that there are people who have enemies riding with them. Who can they count on when things really get hard? Who has their back? I'm a firm believer that if you are a good friend you will attract good friends. I know it won't be easy but they are out there. It won't hurt to give your friends titles and roles in your mind. Write down who your friends are and identify their role in your life. What do they bring to the table? Are they really an asset or are they a liability? Sometimes we have people around us and we don't really know what purpose they serve. It's easy to get caught up with no-good people in your corner if you don't pay attention. I've even had a couple who have tried to get too close to me but thank God for the gift of discernment.

One thing I've focused on not doing is having people around who make me feel like I need to seek their approval. I've seen situations where people have people around them who they want to like them. They have people around whom they are trying to please or impress. I don't have the energy for that. I need people who push me but not people who I feel I have to impress or compete with. What's the point of having friends if you can't truly be happy for one another? There are times when someone sneaks through the cracks and you think they are genuine but then you realize they only want what you have. People have burned me and I'm sure you have been burned too. I learned from it and it taught to me to keep my circle tight. I don't want to compete with another woman. I don't want someone next to me who is jealous of me in any way. I don't want competition around me. We need to be able to eat together and win together. I want people who will push me up and not pull me down. It's so important to have good people in your corner.

A mistake I think we all can make at times is to push away our friends for a relationship. Sometimes we get so caught up in a relationship that we stop talking to our friends and we isolate ourselves. Then when things get tough we don't know who to call. I do believe that your partner should be your friend but you still have to keep your friends you had before you fell in love. They play a different role in friendship than your partner does. A healthy relationship will allow you to keep your friends around you and be a support system in a different type of way. We want love so bad sometimes that we consume ourselves with it and we forget the love we have with friends. I remember having times when I would be so into my relationship that I would neglect my friends; he was my best friend.

I kept my same best friend but we didn't always spend a lot of time together like we used to. I'm fortunate to have the type of friends I can pick up with like nothing ever happened, but the distance isn't always healthy. I want to do that differently moving forward. I want to make sure that my friends always feel included and wanted in my life. I don't just want to call them when I need them, I want them to be there so they already know what's going on.

Your friends are like your board of directors. They will chime in when needed. They will help you pick yourself up and remind you of your worth. Sometimes you'll have to listen to your friends when you can't hear yourself think. When you lose your way your friends will be there to show you the way.

We can be a bad friend to a good friend at times and it's not fair to our good friends. No one wants someone who runs in out and out of their lives. I want to make sure I'm always consistent with my friends and that I'm filling them up the same way they fill me up. I want to make sure that I can be honest with my friends the same way they can be honest with me. It's not easy for a lot of people to keep it real in such a superficial world but I desire real friendships with real bonds. I don't want to lose that real connection because texting and social media are so popular. If I can't pick up the phone and call my friend then I don't want them to be my friend.

Beware of the fake friends who want to be around you for the wrong reason. Some will want to be around you because of who you are. Some will want to be around you for where you're going. Some will want to be around you to see your pain and your struggles so they can feel better about their lives. It's sad that there is such a thing as fake friends but we have to beware of them. I don't trust everyone I meet and I'm very skeptical of adding new people to my life too frequently. Some new people are needed but we have to be very selective of who we let enter our circle. One wrong person in your circle could ruin your life forever. There are so many people who don't value real friendship and they only look at it for the opportunity to gain something. It's sad but it's true and we have to be aware of that fact. My focus is to always be a good friend. I want to give what I want to receive. I still have some of my same friends from the fourth grade and I have a few new ones who make me feel as if they have been around since then. I want to make sure that I'm filling my friends up and that I'm strengthening my circle. I don't ever want to drop the ball in my friendships. Friendships are too valuable to waste.

Who in your life is pushing you to be better? Who is in your circle? Evaluate those people and make sure they are adding to your life. Make sure that you are happier with them around. Make sure that your friends aren't competing with you or jealous of you. You don't owe anyone anything if they don't add something to your life. Adding something doesn't mean money or material things. They should be adding the intangible things in life, the things that money can't buy. If you can't identify what a person brings to the table then they probably need to be removed from your life. You can't get to the top if you're carrying people all the time. You need people who will climb with you and encourage you as you go.

Outside of having your friends, you have to be sure that the person you call your significant other is truly a friend. It's so important that you have a real bond with your partner and that it's not just about sex, lust, and convenience. You have to truly be friends if you want it to work. Your partner shouldn't be your only friend but your partner should be one of your best friends if you plan for it to work. You should be able to talk about anything and to build a stronger bond with every passing day. If you can't talk openly to your partner then you're with the wrong person. The foundation won't be strong enough to hold you up. The conversation and the friendship shouldn't be just one-sided. You maybe can talk to them because you talk a lot, but does your partner talk to you as well? That's what you have to come to terms with. Make sure the person you want to spend your life with can speak into your life and encourage you to be better and to do more. Sex isn't enough in a relationship. Sexiness isn't enough. There has to be more there and it has to be built on friendship. If there is no friendship, there is no relationship. You should be able to lie in bed and talk for hours without having sex. The relationship shouldn't revolve around lust and sex. There has to be an intellectual connection. It doesn't have to be the deepest talks you have but there needs to be a strong communication that can only come from having a real friendship. One thing about friendship is it lasts the test of time when it's real. If the friendship is real you'll know it.

I'm challenging myself and I'm challenging you to build real bonds. I'm evaluating myself and I'm asking myself whether I have been a good friend. I'm going to make it a point to apologize to friends who have been there for me but I dropped the ball on them. I urge you to do the same. Make sure you sew up those relationships because with every passing day the world is becoming more and more crazy and we will need good friends when it's all said and done. There has to be a movement of real friends and the circle has to be protected. There can't be any jealousy, gossiping, and backbiting in the circle of friends. It needs to be a group of genuine people who want to see the person next to them succeed.

At the end of the day make sure you are happy with yourself. You are the nucleus of your circle and if you aren't happy with yourself then you won't be happy with your friends. You have to make sure that your heart and mind are right and that the things you don't want around you aren't already inside of you. It's so easy for us to expect good friends but it's much harder to be a good friend, especially if we aren't where we need to be mentally, spiritually, and emotionally. Keep working on yourself and trust the process that you're in.

Note from the Author:

I really hope this book has been a blessing to you. I'm not trying to win any awards or become the best writer to ever live. I just wanted to share my heart with you, and hopefully the things I've learned along the way will be a confirmation to you. I just want to see people happier and living better lives. Life is hard enough as it is, we don't need anything extra to make it any worse.

I didn't want to put everything in the book because I plan to write more. I hope you'll continue to grow with me. We have to be better, learn more, and strive for greatness. Life is too short to live it beneath the bar. I want to leave a legacy and I hope that you want the same.

Please see my heart through my work. It was not my intention to write a tell-all book or to bash my ex, and I hope you can see that. I don't think we get anywhere by being bitter and harboring hate in our hearts.

I'll be doing tours and I hope to see you on the road!